ELGAR

The Music Makers

OPUS 69

ar

w

Frith Street, London W1V 5TZ

12.95

ODE.

———

We are the music makers,
   And we are the dreamers of dreams,
Wandering by lone sea-breakers,
   And sitting by desolate streams;—
World-losers and world-forsakers,
   On whom the pale moon gleams:
Yet we are the movers and shakers
   Of the world for ever, it seems.

With wonderful deathless ditties
We build up the world's great cities,
   And out of a fabulous story
   We fashion an empire's glory:
One man with a dream, at pleasure,
   Shall go forth and conquer a crown;
And three with a new song's measure
   Can trample a kingdom down.

We, in the ages lying
   In the buried past of the earth,
Built Nineveh with our sighing,
   And Babel itself in our mirth;
And o'erthrew them with prophesying
   To the old of the new world's worth;
For each age is a dream that is dying,
   Or one that is coming to birth.

A breath of our inspiration
Is the life of each generation ;
   A wondrous thing of our dreaming
   Unearthly, impossible seeming—
The soldier, the king, and the peasant
   Are working together in one,
Till our dream shall become their present,
   And their work in the world be done.

They had no vision amazing
Of the goodly house they are raising ;
   They had no divine foreshowing
   Of the land to which they are going :
But on one man's soul it hath broken,
   A light that doth not depart ;
And his look, or a word he hath spoken,
   Wrought flame in another man's heart

And therefore to-day is thrilling
With a past day's late fulfilling ;
   And the multitudes are enlisted
   In the faith that their fathers resisted
And, scorning the dream of to-morrow,
   Are bringing to pass, as they may,
In the world, for its joy or its sorrow,
   The dream that was scorned yesterday.

But we, with our dreaming and singing,
   Ceaseless and sorrowless we !
The glory about us clinging
   Of the glorious futures we see,
Our souls with high music ringing :
   O men ! it must ever be
That we dwell, in our dreaming and singing,
   A little apart from ye.

For we are afar with the dawning
   And the suns that are not yet high,
And out of the infinite morning
   Intrepid you hear us cry—
How, spite of your human scorning,
   Once more God's future draws nigh,
And already goes forth the warning
   That ye of the past must die.

Great hail! we cry to the comers
   From the dazzling unknown shore;
Bring us hither your sun and summers,
   And renew our world as of yore;
You shall teach us your song's new numbers,
   And things that we dreamed not before:
Yea, in spite of a dreamer who slumbers,
   And a singer who sings no more.

ARTHUR O'SHAUGHNESSY.

The words are printed by permission of the Rev. Canon Deacon.

THE MUSIC MAKERS.

A. O'Shaughnessy.

Edward Elgar, Op. 69.

13704

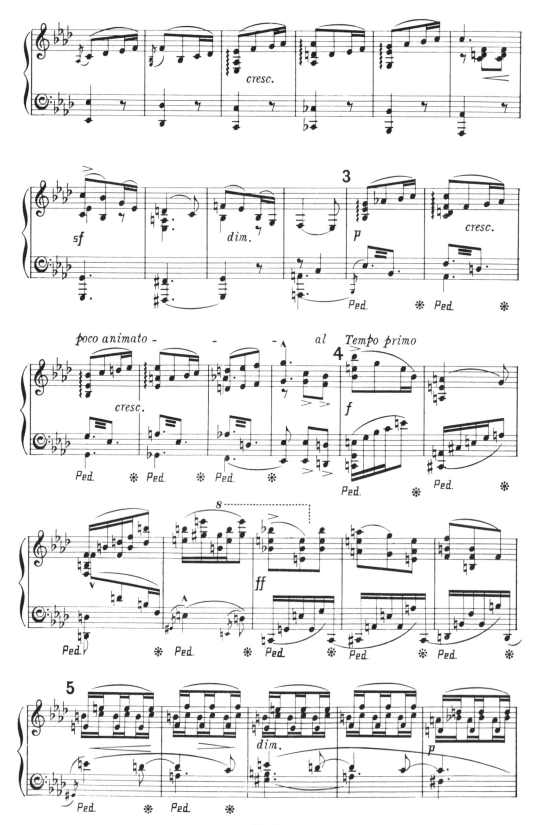

4

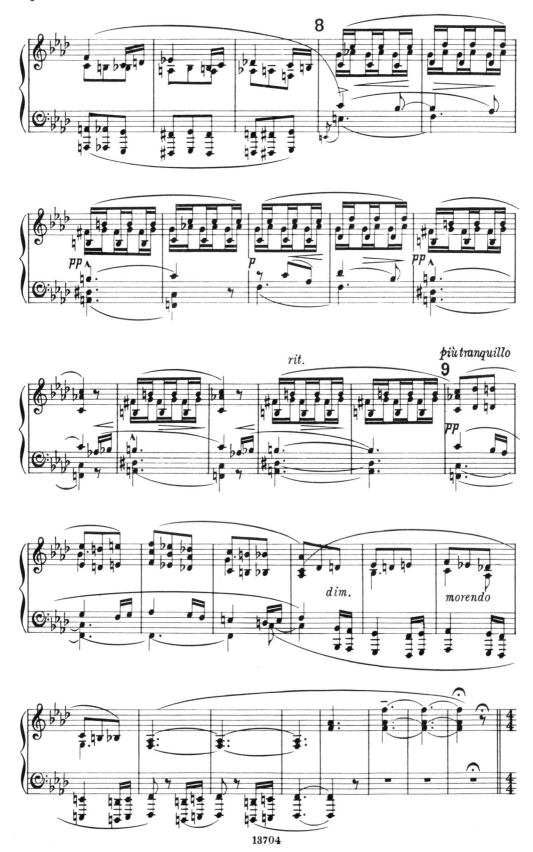

10

12

14

22

can tramp-le a king-dom down.

down, can tramp-le a king-dom down.

can tramp-le a king-dom down.

can tramp-le a king-dom down.

(Drums.)

più lento

27

Ba - bel it - self in our mirth, in our

Ba - bel it - self in our mirth, in our

Ba - bel it - self, Ba - bel it - self in our mirth, in our

mirth, And Ba - bel it - self in our

mirth, in our

mirth, in our

mirth, in our mirth, in our

mirth, in our mirth, in our

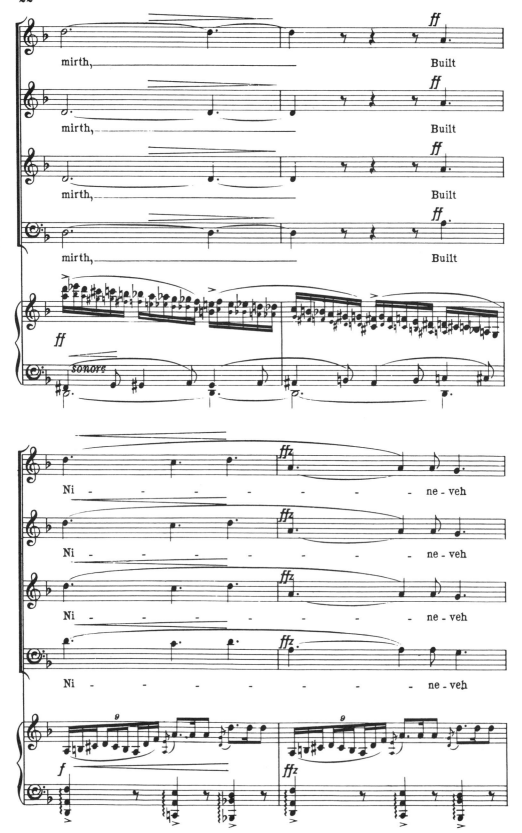

42

Poco più mosso.

45

allargando

45

allargando

46

dream ___   shall ___ become   their pre - ___ - sent.

dream ___   shall ___ become   their pre - ___ - sent.

shall ___ become   their pre - ___ - sent, ___

And their work   in the world ___   be   done.___

And their work   in the world ___   be   done.___

rit. e dim.

Ped.

42

13704

44

13704

VII 19 17

46

54

13704

56

58

62

72

72

13704

64

66

13704

13704

80

You shall teach us your

In our dream-ing and sing - - -

dream-ing and sing - ing, sing - - -

dream - - ing, in our dream-ing and sing - - -

dream - - ing, in our dream-ing and sing - - -

96

largamente   a tempo

song's new numbers, And things that we dreamed not be-fore:

- - ing, O men! it must ev - er be That

- - ing, O men! it must ev - er be That

- - ing, O men! it must ev - er be That

- - ing, O men! it must ev - er be That

96 largamente

86

103 Come prima, ma più lento.

(Judge's Walk, N.W. 1912.)

Printed and bound in Great Britain by
Caligraving Limited Thetford Norfolk

11/00 (38846)